southwestern cooking

Jo Richardson

p

This is a Parragon Publishing Book
First published in 2004

Parragon Publishing
Queen Street House
4 Queen Street
Bath BA1 1HE
United Kingdom

Produced by
The Bridgewater Book Company
Lewes, East Sussex
United Kingdom BN7 2N2

Photographer Emma Neish
Home Economist Joy Skipper

ISBN 1-40543-647-6

Printed in China

NOTE This book uses imperial, metric, or US cup measurements. Follow the same units of
measurement throughout; do not mix imperial and metric. All spoon measurements are level:
teaspoons are assumed to be 5 ml, and tablespoons are assumed to be 15 ml. Unless otherwise
stated, milk is assumed to be whole, eggs, and individual vegetables such as carrots are
medium, and pepper is freshly ground black pepper.

The times given for each recipe are an approximate guide only. The preparation times may
differ according to the techniques used by different people and the cooking times may vary
as a result of the type of oven used. Ovens should be preheated to the specified temperature.
If using a fan-assisted oven, check the manufacturer's instructions for adjusting the time
and temperature.

Recipes using raw eggs should be avoided by infants, the elderly, pregnant women,
convalescents, and anyone suffering from an illness.

contents

Southwestern cooking is border food, gastronomically uniting Texas to the north with Mexico to the south. It is also a fusion food, embracing ancient Aztec, Spanish, Native American, and cowboy influences.

Tortillas, refried beans, salsa, guacamole, and sour cream—these are the staples of southwestern cooking. Then there are the chilies, as in hot, hotter, and hottest. However, in this book you will discover that southwestern cooking is not entirely about heat. Aromatic spices such as cumin combine with coriander, while sweet-scented cinnamon and chocolate add complexity to both savory and sweet dishes.

Most of the recipes suggest a specific variety of dried or fresh chili to use, but if you can't find these, use any hot or mild, fresh or

introduction

dried chilies available. It is difficult to judge how hot a chili will be from outward appearances, but as a general rule of thumb, the smaller the chili, the hotter it is likely to be. The recipes direct you to "seed" fresh chilies before using, because this reduces their hotness, although the heat is actually contained in the membranes surrounding the seeds. You can, however, opt to leave the seeds in to produce a hotter result.

To reconstitute the delightfully smoky but very hard dried chipotle chili, cook in boiling water for 5 minutes (the powerful fumes can irritate your lungs, throat, and nose, so keep well away or protect your face), then let stand for 30 minutes, or until softened; other dried chilies can just be soaked in very hot water for 10–15 minutes. Always wear protective gloves when handling chilies.

There is strong emphasis on snacks in southwestern cooking, with many characteristic dishes eaten with the fingers, encased in a tortilla, or scooped up on a tortilla chip. This chapter features recipes for finger-food favorites such as quesadillas and empanadas, nachos and tostadas. But there's more to whet the appetite, including spicy soups, seafood specials, and eggs prepared ranch-style.

appetizers
and snacks

Mango, although lusciously fruity, goes wonderfully well with savory ingredients and is enhanced, not masked, by the robust flavorings. The color of its succulent flesh is an added bonus.

shrimp and mango cocktail

ingredients

6 cherry tomatoes
1 large ripe mango
1 fresh mild green chili, seeded and
  finely chopped
juice of 1 lime

1 tbsp chopped fresh cilantro
salt and pepper
14 oz/400 g shelled jumbo shrimp,
  cooked
fresh cilantro, chopped, to garnish

one Place the tomatoes in a heatproof bowl and pour over enough boiling water to cover. Let stand for 1–2 minutes, then remove the tomatoes with a slotted spoon, peel off the skins, and refresh in cold water. Dice the flesh and place in a large, nonmetallic bowl.

two Slice the mango lengthwise on either side of the flat central seed. Peel the 2 mango pieces and cut the flesh into chunks. Slice and peel any remaining flesh around the seed, then cut into chunks. Add to the tomatoes with any juice.

three Add the chili, lime juice, chopped cilantro, and salt and pepper to taste. Cover and let chill in the refrigerator for 2 hours to allow the flavors to develop.

four Remove the dish from the refrigerator. Fold the shrimp gently into the mango mixture and divide between 4 serving dishes. Garnish with chopped cilantro and serve at once.

recommended servings

Serve topped with a spoonful of Cilantro Mayonnaise (see page 67). While you are preparing the mango, whizz up a Frozen Mango Margarita (see page 87) to put you in the mango mood.

prepare 20 minutes, plus 8 hours' chilling
cook 0 minutes *serves* 4

This elegant appetizer couldn't be simpler to make but requires several hours' chilling for the raw fish to "cook" in the lime juice— you can tell that it's done when the fish turns opaque.

ceviche salad

ingredients

1 lb/450 g salmon, red snapper, or sole fillets, skinned and cut into strips or slices
1 small onion, finely chopped
1 fresh jalapeño chili or 2 small fresh mild green chilies, seeded and finely chopped
juice of 3 limes
1 tbsp extra virgin olive oil

1 tbsp chopped fresh cilantro, plus extra to garnish
1 tbsp snipped fresh chives or dill
salt and pepper
2 tomatoes, peeled and diced
1 ripe avocado, pitted, peeled, and thinly sliced
2 tbsp capers, rinsed (optional)

one Place the fish, onion, chili, lime juice, oil, and herbs in a nonmetallic dish and mix together. Cover and let chill in the refrigerator for 8 hours or overnight, stirring occasionally to ensure that the fish is well coated in the marinade.

two When ready to serve, remove the dish from the refrigerator and season to taste with salt and pepper.

three Arrange the fish mixture on a large serving plate with the tomatoes and avocado. Sprinkle the capers over the mixture, and sprinkle with chopped cilantro to garnish.

Note

People with certain diseases (such as diabetes or liver disease) or weakened immune systems should never eat raw fish. The elderly and pregnant women (along with nursing mothers and young children) should also avoid eating raw fish.

recommended servings
To make this dish more substantial, serve on a bed of mixed salad greens. Alternatively, for a more traditional southwestern meal, serve on top of shredded crisp lettuce with homemade Flour Tortillas (see page 51).

prepare 15 minutes, plus 2 hours' chilling
cook 0 minutes   *serves* 4

The richness of this tasty chilled soup is balanced by the sharp injection of lime and Tabasco. An optional dash of tequila adds an extra southwestern kick.

chilled avocado and cilantro soup

ingredients

4 ripe avocados
1 shallot or 2 scallions,
  finely chopped
3½ cups cold chicken or strongly
  flavored vegetable stock
⅔ cup sour cream, plus extra
  to serve

2 tbsp tomato paste
few drops of Tabasco sauce, or to taste
juice of 1 lime, or to taste
1 tbsp tequila (optional)
1 tbsp chopped fresh cilantro, plus
  extra to garnish
salt and pepper

one Cut the avocados in half lengthwise and twist the 2 halves in opposite directions to separate. Stab the pit with the point of a sharp knife and lift out of the avocado.

two Peel, then coarsely chop the avocado halves and place in a food processor or blender with the shallot, stock, sour cream, tomato paste, Tabasco, lime juice, tequila, chopped cilantro, and salt and pepper. Process until smooth, then taste and add more Tabasco, lime juice, and salt and pepper if necessary.

three Transfer the mixture to a large bowl, cover, and let chill in the refrigerator for at least 2 hours, or until thoroughly chilled.

four Divide the soup between 4 chilled serving bowls and serve, topped with a spoonful of sour cream and garnished with extra chopped cilantro.

recommended servings
This is the perfect appetizer for an alfresco lunch or dinner southwestern style. Follow with Tequila-Marinated Beef Steaks (see page 39), cooked in moments on the barbecue. A pitcher of Sangria (see page 93) will complete the summery scene.

Stoke up your energy reserves with a bowl of this hearty soup—both comforting and sustaining. It is also highly economical as well as quick and easy to prepare.

beef and pea soup

ingredients

2 tbsp vegetable oil
1 large onion, finely chopped
2 garlic cloves, finely chopped
1 green bell pepper, seeded and sliced
2 carrots, sliced
14 oz/400 g canned black-eye peas
1 cup fresh ground beef

1 tsp each of ground cumin, chili powder, and paprika
¼ cabbage, sliced
8 oz/225 g tomatoes, peeled and chopped
2½ cups beef stock
salt and pepper

one Heat the oil in a large pan over medium heat. Add the onion and garlic and cook, stirring frequently, for 5 minutes, or until softened. Add the bell pepper and carrots and cook for an additional 5 minutes.

two Meanwhile, drain the peas, reserving the liquid from the can. Place two-thirds of the peas, reserving the remainder, in a food processor or blender with the pea liquid and process until smooth.

three Add the ground beef to the pan and cook, stirring constantly, to break up any lumps, until well browned. Add the spices and cook, stirring, for 2 minutes. Add the cabbage, tomatoes, stock, and puréed peas and season to taste with salt and pepper. Bring to a boil, then reduce the heat, cover, and let simmer for 15 minutes, or until the vegetables are tender.

four Stir in the reserved peas, cover, and let simmer for an additional 5 minutes. Ladle the soup into warmed soup bowls and serve.

recommended servings
To make this snack more substantial, serve with a bowl of tortilla chips or warmed corn tortillas. Devotees of southwestern cuisine may like to make a batch of homemade Flour Tortillas (see page 51) as an accompaniment.

prepare 15 minutes *cook* 35–40 minutes *serves* 4

Spice up your morning with these ranch-style or country-style eggs—an ideal dish for a weekend brunch. You can reduce the number of chilies if it's too early in the morning for a fiery hit.

huevos rancheros

ingredients

2 tbsp butter, bacon fat, or lard

2 onions, finely chopped

2 garlic cloves, finely chopped

2 red or yellow bell peppers, seeded and diced

2 fresh mild green chilies, seeded and finely chopped

4 large ripe tomatoes, peeled and chopped

2 tbsp lemon or lime juice

2 tsp dried oregano

salt and pepper

4 large eggs

3 oz/75 g Cheddar cheese, grated

one Preheat the oven to 350°F/180°C. Heat the butter in a heavy-bottom skillet over medium heat. Add the onions and garlic and cook, stirring frequently, for 5 minutes, or until softened. Add the bell peppers and chilies and cook for 5 minutes, until softened.

two Add the tomatoes, lemon juice, and oregano and season to taste with salt and pepper. Bring to a boil, then reduce the heat, cover, and let simmer for 10 minutes, or until thickened, adding a little more lemon juice if the mixture becomes too dry.

three Transfer the mixture to a large, ovenproof dish. Make 4 hollows in the mixture and break an egg into each. Bake in the preheated oven for 12–15 minutes, or until the eggs are set.

four Sprinkle with grated cheese and return to the oven for 3–4 minutes, or until the cheese has melted. Serve at once.

recommended servings

Choose from southwestern traditional accompaniments, such as Flour Tortillas (see page 51), corn tortillas, or tortilla chips, or conventional breakfast fare, such as toast or English muffins, to mop up the delicious sauce.

prepare 15 minutes *cook* 32–40 minutes *serves* 4

The quesadilla is the southwestern take on a toasted cheese sandwich. Oaxacan cheese, also known as Asadero cheese, is the strictly authentic cheese to use, but mozzarella makes a good alternative.

chorizo and cheese quesadillas

ingredients

4 oz/115 g mozzarella cheese, grated
4 oz/115 g Cheddar cheese, grated
8 oz/225 g cooked chorizo sausage, outer casing removed, or ham, diced
4 scallions, finely chopped

2 fresh green chilies, such as poblano, seeded and finely chopped
salt and pepper
8 Flour Tortillas (see page 51)
vegetable oil, for brushing
lime wedges, to garnish

one Place the cheeses, chorizo, scallions, chilies, and salt and pepper to taste in a bowl and mix together.

two Divide the mixture between 4 flour tortillas, then top with the remaining tortillas.

three Brush a large, nonstick or heavy-bottom skillet with oil and heat over medium heat. Add 1 quesadilla and cook, pressing it down with a spatula, for 4–5 minutes, or until the underside is crisp and lightly browned. Turn over and cook the other side until the cheese is melting. Remove from the skillet and keep warm. Cook the remaining quesadillas individually.

four Cut each quesadilla into quarters, arrange on a warmed serving plate, and serve, garnished with lime wedges.

recommended servings
Serve with a bowl of Guacamole (see page 59) and a salsa of your choice, such as Pico de Gallo Salsa (see page 61), Corn and Red Bell Pepper Salsa (see page 63), or Pineapple and Mango Salsa (see page 65).

"Turnovers" do not sound quite so inviting as "empanadas," but these puff pastry packages are real winners. Their packaging makes them a great portable lunch or picnic food.

chicken and corn empanadas

ingredients

14 oz/400 g cooked chicken, diced

~~14 oz/400 g canned creamed-style~~ bl-
~~corn kernels~~   potato bean

1 small onion, finely chopped

 green chilies

~~8 pimiento-stuffed green olives,~~
~~finely chopped~~   onion

2 tbsp finely chopped fresh cilantro

1 tsp Tabasco sauce, or to taste

1 tsp cinnamon

salt and pepper

12 oz/350 g ready-made puff pastry,
   thawed if frozen

all-purpose flour, for dusting

beaten egg, for sealing and glazing

one Preheat the oven to 400°F/200°C. Place the chicken, corn, onion, olives, cilantro, Tabasco, cinnamon, and salt and pepper to taste in a bowl and mix together.

two Roll out the pastry on a lightly floured counter. Using a 6-inch/15-cm saucer as a guide, cut out 8 circles.

three Place an equal quantity of filling on 1 half of each pastry circle. Brush the edge of each circle with beaten egg, fold the pastry over the filling, and press the edges together to seal. Crimp the edges with a fork and prick the tops.

four Place on a baking sheet, brush with beaten egg, and sprinkle lightly with salt. Bake in the preheated oven for 20 minutes, or until golden brown and piping hot in the center.

recommended servings

Serve these empanadas either straight from the oven or cold with a salad garnish, such as strips of bell pepper, shredded lettuce, and chopped onion. You can also serve them with a salsa of your choice (see pages 61–5).

prepare 10 minutes   *cook* 5–8 minutes   *serves* 6

Who can resist diving into a molten mountain of nachos and biting into that great combination of the soggy, chewy, and crispy? Nachos are so easy to prepare, especially if you use canned refried beans.

nachos

ingredients

6 oz/175 g tortilla chips

1 quantity warmed Refried Beans (see page 55) or 14 oz/400 g canned refried beans, warmed

2 tbsp finely chopped bottled jalapeño chilies

7 oz/200 g canned or bottled pimientos or roasted bell peppers, drained and finely sliced

salt and pepper

4 oz/115 g Gruyère cheese, grated

4 oz/115 g Cheddar cheese, grated

one Preheat the oven to 400°F/200°C.

two Spread the tortilla chips out over the bottom of a large, shallow, oven-proof dish or roasting pan. Cover with the warmed refried beans. Sprinkle over the chilies and pimientos and season to taste with salt and pepper. Mix the cheeses together in a bowl and sprinkle on top.

three Bake in the preheated oven for 5–8 minutes, or until the cheese is bubbling and melted. Serve at once.

recommended servings
The classic accompaniment to nachos is Guacamole (see page 59) and sour cream. Serve with an icy glass of Tequila Sunset (see page 89).

This is another southwestern delight. Replace the ground pork with beef if you prefer and, to save time, use corn chips or nacho chips instead of the cooked tortilla wedges.

pork tostadas

ingredients

1 tbsp vegetable oil, plus extra
  for cooking
1 small onion, finely chopped
2 garlic cloves, finely chopped
1 lb/450 g fresh ground pork
2 tsp ground cumin
2 tsp chili powder, plus extra to garnish

1 tsp ground cinnamon
salt and pepper
6 soft corn tortillas, cut into wedges
to serve
shredded iceberg lettuce
sour cream
finely diced red bell pepper

one Heat 1 tablespoon of oil in a heavy-bottom skillet over medium heat. Add the onion and garlic and cook, stirring frequently, for 5 minutes, or until softened. Increase the heat, add the ground pork, and cook, stirring constantly to break up any lumps, until well browned.

two Add the cumin, chili powder, cinnamon, and salt and pepper to taste and cook, stirring, for 2 minutes. Cover and cook over low heat, stirring occasionally, for 10 minutes.

three Meanwhile, heat a little oil in a nonstick skillet. Add the tortilla wedges, in batches, and cook on both sides until crisp. Drain on paper towels.

four Transfer to a serving plate and top with the pork mixture, followed by the lettuce, a little sour cream, and diced bell pepper. Garnish with a sprinkling of chili powder and serve at once.

recommended servings
Serve with a salsa (see pages 61–65) to add extra flavor, or make up a batch of Taco Sauce (see page 41) to spoon over the pork. Enjoy with Classic Margaritas (see page 87) for a memorable "happy hour."

Here are some of the all-time southwestern favorites, including fajitas, enchiladas and, of course, that legend in a bowl, chili, in authentic border-style form, together with updates on the old classics, such as Spinach and Mushroom Chimichangas (see page 47) and Chili-Shrimp Tacos (see page 41). There are other exotic seafood dishes, alongside that most traditional of southwestern fare: beef steaks.

main courses

This is a typical southwestern-style chili, with chunks of beef rather than ground meat and without beans. Purists would also omit onions. Chocolate—a taste of old Mexico—gives extra depth to the sauce.

lone star chili

ingredients

1 tbsp cumin seeds	4 garlic cloves, finely chopped
1 lb 7 oz/650 g rump steak, cut into 1-inch/2.5-cm cubes	1 tbsp dried oregano
all-purpose flour, well seasoned with salt and pepper, for coating	2 tsp paprika
	4 dried red chilies, such as ancho or pasilla, crushed, or to taste
3 tbsp beef drippings, bacon fat, or vegetable oil	1 large bottle of South American lager
2 onions, finely chopped	4 squares semisweet chocolate

one Dry-fry the cumin seeds in a heavy-bottom skillet over medium heat, shaking the skillet, for 3–4 minutes, or until lightly toasted. Let cool, then grind in a mortar with a pestle. Alternatively, use a coffee grinder reserved for the purpose.

two Toss the beef in the seasoned flour to coat. Melt the fat in a large, heavy-bottom pan. Add the beef, in batches, and cook until browned on all sides. Remove the beef with a slotted spoon and set aside.

three Add the onions and garlic to the pan and cook gently for 5 minutes, or until softened. Add the cumin, oregano, paprika, and chilies and cook, stirring, for 2 minutes. Return the beef to the pan, pour over the lager, then add the chocolate. Bring to a boil, stirring, then reduce the heat, cover, and let simmer for 2–3 hours, or until the beef is very tender, adding more lager if necessary.

recommended servings
Serve with warmed Flour Tortillas (see page 51), or hunks of Chilied Cornbread (see page 53). Hand round a bowl of sour cream to douse the flames and wash it down with additional ice-cold beer of your choice.

This is a stew of southern climes rather than the chilly north, full of warm, sunny flavors. Mexican oregano is rather different to the Mediterranean variety, but the latter still works well here.

spicy pork and vegetable hotchpotch

ingredients

1 lb/450 g lean boneless pork, cut into 1-inch/2.5-cm cubes

all-purpose flour, well seasoned with salt and pepper, for coating

1 tbsp vegetable oil

8 oz/225 g chorizo sausage, outer casing removed, cut into bite-size chunks

1 onion, coarsely chopped

4 garlic cloves, finely chopped

2 celery stalks, chopped

1 cinnamon stick, broken

2 bay leaves

2 tsp allspice

2 carrots, sliced

2–3 fresh red chilis, seeded and finely chopped

6 ripe tomatoes, peeled and chopped

4 cups pork or vegetable stock

2 sweet potatoes, cut into chunks

corn kernels, cut from 1 ear fresh corn

1 tbsp chopped fresh oregano

salt and pepper

fresh oregano sprigs, to garnish

one Toss the pork in the seasoned flour to coat. Heat the oil in a large, heavy-bottom pan or ovenproof casserole. Add the chorizo and lightly brown on all sides. Remove the chorizo with a slotted spoon and set aside.

two Add the pork, in batches, and cook until browned on all sides. Remove the pork with a slotted spoon and set aside. Add the onion, garlic, and celery to the pan and cook for 5 minutes, or until softened.

three Add the cinnamon, bay leaves, and allspice and cook, stirring, for 2 minutes. Add the pork, carrots, chilis, tomatoes, and stock. Bring to a boil, then reduce the heat, cover, and let simmer for 1 hour, or until the pork is tender.

four Return the chorizo to the pan with the sweet potatoes, corn, oregano, and salt and pepper to taste. Cover and let simmer for an additional 30 minutes, or until the vegetables are tender. Serve garnished with oregano sprigs.

recommended servings
Since this dish provides a cornucopia of flavor, plain boiled rice would make a suitable accompaniment. If, however, you are feeding unexpected guests, serve with wedges of Chilied Cornbread (see page 53).

prepare 20 minutes, plus 10 minutes' cooling
cook 50 minutes *serves* 4

Roasting the bell peppers, tomatoes, chilies, and garlic enhances the flavor of this sumptuous seafood medley. You can use any other firm fish fillets or a mixture, if you prefer.

southwestern seafood stew

ingredients

1 each of yellow, red, and orange bell peppers, seeded and quartered	1 lime, finely grated rind and juice of
1 lb/450 g ripe tomatoes	2 tbsp chopped fresh cilantro, plus extra to garnish
2 large fresh mild green chilies, such as poblano	1 bay leaf
6 garlic cloves, peeled	salt and pepper
2 tsp dried oregano or dried mixed herbs	1 lb/450 g red snapper fillets, skinned and cut into chunks
2 tbsp olive oil, plus extra for drizzling	8 oz/225 g raw shrimp, shelled and deveined
1 large onion, finely chopped	8 oz/225 g cleaned squid, cut into rings
2 cups fish, vegetable, or chicken stock	

one Preheat the oven to 400°F/200°C. Place the bell pepper quarters, skin side up, in a roasting pan with the tomatoes, chilies, and garlic. Sprinkle with the dried oregano and drizzle with oil.

two Roast in the preheated oven for 30 minutes, or until the bell peppers are well browned and softened.

three Remove the roasted vegetables from the oven and let stand until cool enough to handle. Peel off the skins from the bell peppers, tomatoes, and chilies and chop the flesh. Finely chop the garlic.

four Heat the oil in a large pan. Add the onion and cook for 5 minutes, or until softened. Add the bell peppers, tomatoes, chilies, garlic, stock, lime rind and juice, chopped cilantro, bay leaf, and salt and pepper to taste. Bring to a boil, then stir in the seafood. Reduce the heat, cover, and let simmer gently for 10 minutes, or until the seafood is just cooked through. Garnish with chopped cilantro before serving.

recommended servings
Warmed Flour Tortillas (see page 51) would make a perfect accompaniment. For an additional touch of luxury, add a spoonful of Cilantro Mayonnaise (see page 67) to each serving of the stew.

prepare 20 minutes, plus 30 minutes' soaking
cook 1 hour 20 minutes *serves* 4

This recipe features a famed sauce, Mole Poblano, renowned for its surprising pairing of chocolate and chili. The result is sumptuous rather than strange, with a deep, rich, mellow quality.

chicken mole poblano

ingredients

3 tbsp olive oil

4 chicken pieces, about 6 oz/175 g each, halved

1 onion, chopped

2 garlic cloves, finely chopped

1 hot dried red chili, such as chipotle, or 2 milder dried chilies, such as ancho, reconstituted (see page 5) and finely chopped

1 tbsp sesame seeds, toasted, plus extra to garnish

1 tbsp chopped almonds

¼ tsp each of ground cinnamon, cumin, and cloves

3 tomatoes, peeled and chopped

2 tbsp raisins

1½ cups chicken stock

1 tbsp peanut butter

1 oz/25 g semisweet chocolate with a high cocoa content, grated, plus extra to garnish

salt and pepper

one Heat 2 tablespoons of the oil in a large skillet. Add the chicken and cook until browned on all sides. Remove the chicken pieces with a slotted spoon and set aside.

two Add the onion, garlic, and chilies and cook for 5 minutes, or until softened. Add the sesame seeds, almonds, and spices and cook, stirring, for 2 minutes. Add the tomatoes, raisins, stock, peanut butter, and chocolate and stir well. Season to taste with salt and pepper and let simmer for 5 minutes.

three Transfer the mixture to a food processor or blender and process until smooth (you may need to do this in batches).

four Return the mixture to the skillet, add the chicken, and bring to a boil. Reduce the heat, cover, and let simmer for 1 hour, or until the chicken is very tender, adding more liquid if necessary.

five Serve garnished with sesame seeds and a little grated chocolate.

recommended servings

Spicy Rice (see page 57) adds color and texture to this dish. Alternatively, serve with warmed Refried Beans (see page 55) and a bowl of Pineapple and Mango Salsa (see page 65) for a light finish to the dish.

This is just about as light as it gets in southwestern cooking—white fish fillets simply seasoned and baked, accompanied by a tropical fruit sauce enlivened with a dash of hot pepper sauce.

fish fillets with papaya sauce

ingredients

4 white fish fillets, such as sea bass, sole, or cod, about 6 oz/175 g each, skinned
olive oil, for drizzling
juice of 1 lime
2 tbsp chopped fresh cilantro
salt and pepper

lime wedges, to garnish
papaya sauce
1 large ripe papaya
1 tbsp freshly squeezed orange juice
1 tbsp freshly squeezed lime juice
1 tbsp olive oil
1–2 tsp Tabasco sauce

one Preheat the oven to 350°F/180°C. Place the fish in a shallow ovenproof dish. Drizzle with oil and squeeze over the lime juice. Sprinkle the chopped cilantro over the fish and season to taste with salt and pepper.

two Cover the dish tightly with foil and bake in the preheated oven for 15–20 minutes, or until the fish is just flaking.

three Meanwhile, to make the sauce, halve the papaya and scoop out the seeds. Peel the halves and chop the flesh. Place the flesh in a food processor or blender and add the orange and lime juices, oil, and Tabasco to taste. Process until smooth.

four Transfer the sauce to a pan and heat through gently for 3–4 minutes. Season to taste with salt and pepper.

five Serve the fish fillets, in their cooking juices, with the sauce spooned over, garnished with lime wedges.

recommended servings
Spicy Rice (see page 57), together with a touch of something rich and creamy, such as Cilantro Mayonnaise (see page 67), make ideal accompaniments.

prepare 10 minutes, plus 2 hours' marinating
and 30 minutes' standing *cook* 6–8 minutes *serves* 4

Now it's barbecue time, southwestern style, with a marinade
guaranteed to make your meat melt in the mouth. If the weather is
inclement, then cook the steaks under a preheated hot broiler.

tequila-marinated beef steaks

ingredients

2 tbsp olive oil

3 tbsp tequila

3 tbsp freshly squeezed orange juice

1 tbsp freshly squeezed lime juice

3 garlic cloves, crushed

2 tsp chili powder

2 tsp ground cumin

1 tsp dried oregano

salt and pepper

4 sirloin steaks

one Place the oil, tequila, orange and lime juices, garlic, chili powder, cumin, oregano, and salt and pepper to taste in a large, shallow, nonmetallic dish and mix together. Add the steaks and turn to coat in the marinade. Cover and let chill in the refrigerator for at least 2 hours or overnight, turning occasionally.

two Preheat the barbecue and oil the grill rack. Let the steaks return to room temperature, then remove from the marinade. Cook over hot coals for 3–4 minutes on each side for medium, or longer according to taste, basting frequently with the marinade. Serve at once.

recommended servings
To add color and texture to this dish serve with a bowl of Corn and Red Bell Pepper Salsa (see page 63), and some crispy cooked, preblanched potato slices or chunks. Serve with Classic Margaritas (see page 87).

This is a gourmet, not to say healthy take on a trusty southwestern favorite—ideal for an informal dinner party. Use cooked shrimp and just heat through gently in the sauce for an everyday option.

chili-shrimp tacos

ingredients

1 lb 5 oz/600 g raw shrimp, shelled
  and deveined
2 tbsp chopped fresh flatleaf parsley
12 tortilla shells
scallions, chopped, to garnish
taco sauce
1 tbsp olive oil
1 onion, finely chopped
1 green bell pepper, seeded and diced
1–2 fresh hot green chilies, such
  as jalapeño, seeded and finely
  chopped

3 garlic cloves, crushed
1 tsp ground cumin
1 tsp ground coriander
1 tsp brown sugar
1 lb/450 g ripe tomatoes, peeled
  and coarsely chopped
juice of ½ lemon
salt and pepper
to serve
sour cream

one Preheat the oven to 350°F/180°C. To make the sauce, heat the oil in a deep skillet over medium heat. Add the onion and cook for 5 minutes, or until softened. Add the bell pepper and chilies and cook for 5 minutes. Add the garlic, cumin, coriander, and sugar and cook the sauce for an additional 2 minutes, stirring.

two Add the tomatoes, lemon juice, and salt and pepper to taste. Bring to a boil, then reduce the heat and let simmer for 10 minutes.

three Stir in the shrimp and parsley, cover, and cook gently for 5–8 minutes, or until the shrimp are pink and tender.

four Meanwhile, place the tortilla shells, open-side down, on a baking sheet. Warm in the preheated oven for 2–3 minutes.

five To serve, spoon the shrimp mixture into the tortilla shells and top with a spoonful of sour cream.

recommended servings
Serve with a colorful combination of salsas, such as Pineapple and Mango Salsa (see page 65) and Corn and Red Bell Pepper Salsa (see page 63). Finish with a pitcher of Sangria (see page 93).

prepare 15 minutes, plus 2–3 hours' marinating
cook 12–15 minutes *serves* 4

The secret of fajita success lies in the marinating of the meat prior
to quick cooking. It may take a little forward planning but very
little extra effort for a far superior result.

chicken fajitas

ingredients

3 tbsp olive oil, plus extra for drizzling
3 tbsp maple syrup or honey
1 tbsp red wine vinegar
2 garlic cloves, crushed
2 tsp dried oregano
1–2 tsp dried red pepper flakes

salt and pepper
4 skinless, boneless chicken breasts
2 red bell peppers, seeded and cut into
 1-inch/2.5-cm strips
8 Flour Tortillas (see page 51), warmed

one Place the oil, maple syrup, vinegar, garlic, oregano, pepper flakes, and
salt and pepper to taste in a large, shallow dish or bowl and mix together.

two Slice the chicken across the grain into slices 1 inch/2.5 cm thick. Toss in
the marinade until well coated. Cover and let chill in the refrigerator for
2–3 hours, turning occasionally.

three Heat a grill pan until hot. Lift the chicken slices from the
marinade with a slotted spoon, lay on the grill pan, and cook over medium-
high heat for 3–4 minutes on each side, or until cooked through. Remove the
chicken to a warmed serving plate and keep warm.

four Add the bell peppers, skin-side down, to the grill pan and cook for
2 minutes on each side. Transfer to the serving plate.

five Serve at once with the warmed tortillas to be used as wraps.

recommended servings
Serve with Guacamole (see page 59), sour cream,
Pico de Gallo Salsa (see page 61), and shredded iceberg
lettuce to put in the fajitas. Accompany with Refried
Beans (see page 55) or Spicy Rice (see page 57).

This is a dish for those seriously committed to comfort eating. It would be equally effective with good-quality ground beef in place of the pieces of beef, if you prefer.

beef enchiladas

ingredients

2 tbsp olive oil, plus extra for oiling
2 large onions, thinly sliced
1 lb 4 oz/550 g lean beef, cut into bite-size pieces
1 tbsp ground cumin
1–2 tsp cayenne pepper, or to taste
1 tsp paprika

salt and pepper
8 soft corn tortillas
1 quantity Taco Sauce (see page 41), warmed, and thinned with a little water if necessary
8 oz/225 g Cheddar cheese, grated

one Preheat the oven to 350°F/180°C. Oil a large, rectangular baking dish.

two Heat the oil in a large skillet over low heat. Add the onions and cook for 10 minutes, or until soft and golden. Remove with a slotted spoon and set aside.

three Increase the heat to high, add the beef, and cook, stirring, for 2–3 minutes, or until browned on all sides. Reduce the heat to medium, add the spices and salt and pepper to taste, and cook, stirring constantly, for 2 minutes.

four Warm each tortilla in a lightly oiled nonstick skillet for 15 seconds on each side, then dip each, in turn, in the sauce. Top with a little of the beef, onions, and grated cheese and roll up.

five Place seam-side down in the prepared baking dish, top with the remaining sauce and grated cheese, and bake in the preheated oven for 30 minutes. Serve at once.

recommended servings

Serve with a garnish of shredded iceberg lettuce, finely chopped red onion, and cubes of firm avocado, tossed in lime juice to prevent discoloration. Accompany with a salsa (see pages 61–5) and Refried Beans (see page 55).

These crisp deep-fried packages are universally appealing and are speedy to make. For an alternative meat filling, try the Lone Star Chili (see page 29) topped with chopped onion and grated cheese.

spinach and mushroom chimichangas

ingredients

2 tbsp olive oil

1 large onion, finely chopped

8 oz/225 g small mushrooms, finely sliced

2 fresh mild green chilies, seeded and finely chopped

2 garlic cloves, finely chopped

5⅝ cups spinach leaves, torn into pieces if large

6 oz/175 g Cheddar cheese, grated

8 Flour Tortillas (see page 51), warmed

vegetable oil, for deep-frying

one Heat the oil in a large, heavy-bottom skillet. Add the onion and cook over medium heat for 5 minutes, or until softened.

two Add the mushrooms, chilies, and garlic and cook for 5 minutes, or until the mushrooms are lightly browned. Add the spinach and cook, stirring, for 1–2 minutes, or until just wilted. Add the cheese and stir until just melted.

three Spoon an equal quantity of the mixture into the center of each tortilla. Fold in 2 opposite sides of each tortilla to cover the filling, then roll up to enclose it completely.

four Heat the oil for deep-frying in a deep-fryer or large, deep pan to 350–375°F/180–190°C, or until a cube of bread browns in 30 seconds. Deep-fry the chimichangas 2 at a time, turning once, for 5–6 minutes, or until crisp and golden. Drain on paper towels before serving.

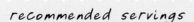

recommended servings

Serve with a spoonful of Guacamole (see page 59) and sour cream, a little chopped, seeded fresh tomato with chopped onion, and a side dish of Spicy Rice (see page 57). Enjoy with a Tequila Sunset (see page 89).

No southwestern meal would be complete without an array of extra dishes on the side and in this chapter all the essentials are featured to ensure success. There is a range of salsas, from fiery to fruity, to perk up your main course, spiced beans and fragrant rice to provide additional flavor interest, as well as tortillas and cornbread for mopping up all those delicious juices.

side dishes and accompaniments

prepare 40 minutes, plus 15 minutes' resting
cook 24–48 minutes *makes* 12

Fresh, homemade flour tortillas are, unsurprisingly, rather more delicious than the store-bought variety, but the latter definitely win over on convenience when required in other southwestern dishes.

flour tortillas

ingredients

2¼ cups all-purpose flour, plus extra
   for dusting
1 tsp salt
½ tsp baking powder

2¾ oz/75 g shortening or white
   vegetable fat, diced
about ½ cup hot water

one Sift the flour, salt, and baking powder into a large bowl. Add the shortening and rub it in with your fingertips until the mixture resembles fine bread crumbs. Add enough water to form a soft dough.

two Turn out the dough on to a lightly floured counter and knead until smooth. Divide the dough into 12 pieces and shape each into a ball. Cover with a clean dish towel and let rest for 15 minutes.

three Roll out 1 ball at a time, keeping the remainder of the dough covered, into an 7-inch/18-cm circle. Stack the tortillas between sheets of nonstick parchment paper.

four Heat a grill pan or large, heavy-bottom skillet over medium-high heat. Cook 1 tortilla at a time for 1–2 minutes on each side, or until lightly browned in places and puffed up. Serve warm.

recommended servings

As well as playing a leading role in many southwestern mainstays, flour tortillas are great with soups and stews such as Beef and Pea Soup (page 15), Southwestern Seafood Stew (see page 33), and Lone Star Chili (see page 29).

This is authentic chuck-wagon fare that will satisfy any hearty appetite. If you fancy a cheesy version, add ¾ cup grated Cheddar cheese to the mixture and sprinkle extra on top before baking.

chilied cornbread

ingredients

scant 1 cup cornmeal
scant ½ cup all-purpose flour
3 tsp baking powder
1 small onion, finely chopped
1–2 fresh green chilies, such as
  jalapeño, seeded and chopped

4 tbsp corn or vegetable oil
4½ oz/125 g canned creamed-style
  corn kernels
1 cup sour cream
2 eggs, beaten

one Preheat the oven to 350°F/180°C.

two Place the cornmeal, flour, and baking powder in a large bowl, then stir in the onion and chili.

three Heat the oil in a 9-inch/23-cm heavy-bottom skillet with a heatproof handle, tipping the skillet to coat the bottom and sides with the oil.

four Make a well in the center of the ingredients in the bowl. Add the corn, sour cream, and eggs, then pour in the hot oil from the skillet. Stir lightly until combined. Pour into the hot skillet and smooth the surface.

five Bake in the preheated oven for 35–40 minutes, or until a wooden toothpick inserted into the center comes out clean. Cut into wedges and serve warm from the skillet.

recommended servings

This robust accompaniment needs a main course that measures up to its stature. Serve it with Lone Star Chili (see page 29) or Spicy Pork and Vegetable Hotchpotch (see page 31).

prepare 10 minutes, plus 8 hours' soaking
cook 2¼ hours *serves* 4

Frijoles refritos, to give them their proper name, are simply a southwestern must and, while you can depend on the canned variety, why not enjoy the real thing now and again?

refried beans

ingredients

1⅓ cups dried pinto beans, soaked overnight and drained

2 onions, 1 quartered and 1 chopped

1 chopped and 1 whole bay leaf

1 fresh thyme sprig

1 dried red chili, such as ancho

3 tbsp olive oil

2 tsp ground cumin

3 oz/85 g Cheddar cheese, grated (optional)

one Place the beans in a large pan with the quartered onion, the herbs, and chili. Pour over enough cold water to cover and bring to a boil. Reduce the heat, cover, and let simmer gently for 2 hours, or until the beans are very tender.

two Drain the beans, reserving the cooking liquid, and discard the onion, herbs, and chili.

three Place two-thirds of the beans with the cooking liquid in a food processor or blender and process until coarsely blended.

four Heat the oil in a heavy-bottom skillet over medium heat. Add the chopped onion and cook for 10 minutes, or until soft and golden. Add the cumin and cook, stirring, for 2 minutes. Stir in the puréed and reserved beans and cook, stirring constantly, until the liquid reduces and the mixture thickens. Stir in the grated cheese, if using, and cook, stirring, until melted. Serve at once.

recommended servings
You can ladle these on the side, without the cheese, of many of the main courses in the book, such as the Chicken Mole Poblano (see page 35) or the Beef Enchiladas (see page 45).

prepare 15 minutes, plus 5 minutes' standing
cook 30 minutes *serves* 4

Both full of color and flavor, this is so much more inviting than plain boiled rice. Add some canned red kidney or black-eye peas with the stock for a more substantial alternative.

spicy rice

ingredients

3 tbsp olive oil
6 scallions, chopped
1 celery stalk, finely chopped
3 garlic cloves, finely chopped
2 green bell peppers, seeded
  and chopped
corn kernels, cut from 1
  ear fresh corn

2 fresh mild green chilies, seeded and
  finely chopped
generous 1¼ cups long-grain rice
2 tsp ground cumin
2½ cups chicken or vegetable stock
2 tbsp chopped fresh cilantro
salt and pepper
fresh cilantro sprigs, to garnish

one Heat the oil in a large, heavy-bottom pan over medium heat. Add the scallions, celery, and garlic and cook for 5 minutes, or until softened. Add the bell peppers, corn, and chilies and cook for 5 minutes.

two Add the rice and cumin and cook, stirring to coat the grains in the oil, for 2 minutes.

three Stir in the stock and half the chopped cilantro and bring to a boil. Reduce the heat, cover, and let simmer for 15 minutes, or until nearly all the liquid has been absorbed and the rice is just tender.

four Remove from the heat and fluff up with a fork. Stir in the remaining chopped cilantro and season to taste with salt and pepper. Let stand, covered, for 5 minutes before serving. Serve garnished with cilantro sprigs.

recommended servings

Serve as an accompaniment to Fish Fillets with Papaya Sauce (see page 37), or Refried Beans (see page 55) and Chicken Fajitas (see page 43).

There are as many versions of this dish as there are cooks, but a good result always depends on using quality, ripe avocados. Mashing rather than puréeing gives control over the texture.

guacamole

ingredients

2 large, ripe avocados

juice of 1 lime, or to taste

2 tsp olive oil

½ onion, finely chopped

1 fresh green chili, such as poblano, seeded and finely chopped

1 garlic clove, crushed

¼ tsp ground cumin

1 tbsp chopped fresh cilantro, plus extra to garnish (optional)

salt and pepper

one Cut the avocados in half lengthwise and twist the 2 halves in opposite directions to separate. Stab the pit with the point of a sharp knife and lift out.

two Peel, then coarsely chop the avocado halves and place in a nonmetallic bowl. Squeeze over the lime juice and add the oil.

three Mash the avocados with a fork until the desired consistency—either chunky or smooth. Blend in the onion, chili, garlic, cumin, and chopped cilantro, then season to taste with salt and pepper.

four Transfer to a serving dish and serve at once, to avoid discoloration, sprinkled with extra chopped cilantro, if liked.

recommended servings

This relish teams well with sour cream and salsa in tortilla-based dishes, such as Chorizo and Cheese Quesadillas (see page 19), fajitas (see page 43), and chimichangas (see page 47).

prepare 10 minutes, plus 30 minutes' chilling
cook 0 minutes *serves* 4–6

This is the most famous southwestern salsa, its name translating as "rooster's beak," so-called, allegedly, because it was traditionally eaten between the thumb and index finger, pecking-style.

pico de gallo salsa

ingredients

3 large, ripe tomatoes
½ red onion, finely chopped
1 large fresh green chili, such as
  jalapeño, seeded and
  finely chopped

2 tbsp chopped fresh cilantro
juice of 1 lime, or to taste
salt and pepper

one Halve the tomatoes, scoop out and discard the seeds, and dice the flesh. Place the flesh in a large, nonmetallic bowl.

two Add the onion, chili, chopped cilantro and lime juice. Season to taste with salt and pepper and stir gently to combine.

three Cover and let chill in the refrigerator for at least 30 minutes to allow the flavors to develop before serving.

recommended servings
This fiery salsa is especially good with tortilla dishes, such as Chorizo and Cheese Quesadillas (see page 19) and chimichangas (see page 47), or it can be spread over plain broiled and grilled meat and poultry.

prepare 10 minutes, plus 30 minutes' chilling
cook 0 minutes *serves* 4–6

This salsa has lots of natural texture and a sweet-and-sour taste. Use a large fresh green chili in place of the bottled chilies if you prefer, or use half a red onion instead of the scallions.

corn and red bell pepper salsa

ingredients

1 lb/450 g canned corn kernels

1 large red bell pepper, diced

1 garlic clove, crushed

1–2 tbsp finely chopped bottled
   jalapeño chilies, or to taste

4 scallions, finely chopped

2 tbsp lemon juice

1 tbsp olive oil

1 tbsp chopped fresh cilantro

salt

one Drain the corn and place in a large, nonmetallic bowl.

two Add the red bell pepper, garlic, chilies, scallions, lemon juice, oil, and chopped cilantro, then season to taste with salt and stir well to combine.

three Cover and let chill in the refrigerator for at least 30 minutes to allow the flavors to develop before serving.

recommended servings

Try serving this with the Chicken Fajitas (see page 43) or beef dishes, such as Tequila-Marinated Beef Steaks (see page 39) and Beef Enchiladas (see page 45).

Full of tropical fruit flavors, this exotic salsa provides a lively flavor contrast to robust savory southwestern fare. You could substitute a papaya for the mango for a slightly different taste experience.

pineapple and mango salsa

ingredients

½ ripe pineapple
1 ripe mango
2 tbsp chopped fresh mint
2 tsp brown sugar
juice of 1 lime

1–2 tsp Tabasco sauce or Habañero
 sauce, or to taste
1 large tomato, seeded and diced
salt

one Slice the pineapple, then peel the slices and remove the cores. Dice the flesh and place in a nonmetallic bowl with any juice.

two Slice the mango lengthwise on either side of the flat central seed. Peel the 2 mango pieces and dice the flesh. Slice and peel any remaining flesh around the seed, then dice. Add to the pineapple with any juice.

three Add the chopped mint, sugar, lime juice, Tabasco, and tomato, then season to taste with salt and stir well to combine. Cover and let chill in the refrigerator for at least 30 minutes to allow the flavors to develop. Stir again before serving.

recommended servings
Bring an extra touch of sophistication to the Chicken Mole Poblano (see page 35) with a spoonful of this salsa on the side. It will also add vibrancy to the Chicken and Corn Empanadas (see page 21).

prepare 10 minutes, plus 30 minutes' chilling
cook 0 minutes *serves* 4

Making your own mayonnaise is very straightforward, especially with a food processor or blender. The addition of a green chili gives it that traditional southwestern flavor.

cilantro mayonnaise

ingredients

1 egg

2 tsp prepared mustard

½ tsp salt

squeeze of lemon juice

2 tbsp chopped fresh cilantro

1 fresh mild green chili, seeded and
 finely chopped

1½ cups olive oil

one Place the egg in a food processor or blender, add the mustard and salt and process for 30 seconds.

two Add the lemon juice, cilantro, and chili and process briefly.

three With the motor still running, add the olive oil through the feeder tube in a thin, steady stream. The mixture will thicken after half the oil has been added.

four Continue adding the remaining oil until it is all absorbed. Transfer to a serving bowl, cover, and let chill in the refrigerator for 30 minutes to allow the flavors to develop before serving.

Note

Recipes using raw eggs should be avoided by infants, the elderly, pregnant women, convalescents, and anyone suffering from an illness.

recommended servings

This mayonnaise goes well with the Shrimp and Mango Cocktail (see page 9). Try a spoonful with the Fish Fillets with Papaya Sauce (see page 37), or use it instead of the sour cream in the Chili-Shrimp Tacos (see page 41).

To satisfy the inevitable desire for something sweet after a surfeit of southwestern savory dishes, choose from this special selection of cookies and cakes, traditional Mexican deep-fried fritters and chilled desserts. Along with luscious tropical and tangy citrus fruits, pecans, and scented cinnamon, seductive semisweet chocolate also features strongly, as well as tequila and even chili!

For drinks, think tequila. For tequila, think Margarita. And here is the definitive formula, along with a recipe for a frozen, fresh fruit variation. But tequila can also appear in a mellower mode, its mature, golden form teamed with tropical fruit and coconut milk to make a sumptuous cocktail, or combined with Kahlúa and cream to make a spectacular liqueur coffee.

desserts, bakes, and drinks

This silken dessert with its crunchy caramel topping is traditional in Mexico and is commonly known as "flan." The addition of chocolate makes it even more luxurious and tempting.

mexican chocolate crème caramel

ingredients

generous ½ cup granulated sugar
4 tbsp water
2½ cups milk
2 oz/55 g semisweet chocolate, grated

4 eggs
2 tbsp superfine sugar
1 tsp vanilla extract

one Preheat the oven to 325°F/160°C. Place a 4-cup soufflé dish in the oven to heat.

two Place the granulated sugar and water in a heavy-bottom pan over low heat. Stir until the sugar has dissolved. Bring to a boil, without stirring, and boil until caramelized. Pour into the hot dish, tipping it to coat the bottom and sides. Let cool.

three Place the milk and grated chocolate in a separate pan and heat, stirring occasionally, until the chocolate has dissolved.

four Meanwhile, beat the eggs and superfine sugar together in a bowl with a wooden spoon. Gradually beat in the chocolate milk. Add the vanilla extract. Strain into the prepared dish.

five Stand the dish in a roasting pan and fill the pan with enough lukewarm water to come halfway up the sides of the dish. Bake in the preheated oven for 1 hour, or until set. Let cool, then invert onto a serving plate. Let chill in the refrigerator before serving.

recommended servings

Delicious on its own, perhaps with some chocolate curls for a special occasion, you could also serve it with some ripe berries, such as raspberries or blueberries, or even sliced banana for a comforting treat.

prepare 20 minutes *cook* 35–40 minutes *serves* 4

There are many variations of this easy pudding, called *capirotada*, which turns a loaf of bread into an irresistible dessert. Use strained cottage cheese in place of the Cheddar for a lighter version.

mexican bread pudding

ingredients

2 oz/55 g butter, plus extra for greasing
1½ cups water
generous 1 cup brown sugar
1 cinnamon stick, broken
1 tsp ground anise
⅓ cup raisins

10 small slices bread
¾ cup shelled pecans, toasted
  and chopped
½ cup slivered almonds, toasted
6 oz/175 g mild Cheddar cheese, grated

one Preheat the oven to 375°F/190°C. Generously grease an ovenproof dish.

two Heat the water, sugar, cinnamon stick, and anise in a pan over medium heat and stir constantly until the sugar has dissolved. Add the raisins and let simmer for 5 minutes without stirring.

three Spread butter onto one side of each bread slice and arrange buttered-side up on a baking sheet. Bake in the preheated oven for 5 minutes, or until golden brown. Turn over and bake the other side for 5 minutes.

four Line the base of the ovenproof dish with half the toast. Sprinkle over half the nuts and grated cheese. Remove and discard the cinnamon stick from the raisin mixture, then spoon half of the raisin mixture over the toast. Top with the remaining toast, nuts, grated cheese, and raisin mixture.

five Bake in the preheated oven for 20–25 minutes, or until set and golden brown on top.

recommended servings

Serve with light cream poured over for a midmorning or teatime indulgence, with a cup of strong coffee.
Alternatively, hold the cream and serve with a glass of Southwestern Coffee (see page 95) for a dinnertime finale.

prepare 25 minutes, plus 3 minutes' cooling
cook 20 minutes *serves* 4

This southwestern-style doughnut is looks rather more appealing than its traditional relative, since the dough is piped into lengths, which twist into a variety of interesting shapes when deep-fried.

churros

ingredients

1 cup water
3 oz/85 g butter or shortening, diced
2 tbsp brown sugar
finely grated rind of 1 small orange
  (optional)
pinch of salt
1⅛ cups all-purpose flour, well sifted

1 tsp ground cinnamon, plus extra
  for dusting
1 tsp vanilla extract
2 eggs
vegetable oil, for deep-frying
superfine sugar, for dusting

one Heat the water, butter, brown sugar, orange rind, if using, and salt in a heavy-bottom pan over medium heat until the butter has melted.

two Add the flour, all at once, the cinnamon, and vanilla extract, then remove the pan from the heat and beat rapidly until the mixture pulls away from the side of the pan.

three Let cool slightly, then beat in the eggs, one at a time, beating well after each addition, until the mixture is thick and smooth. Spoon into a pastry bag fitted with a wide star tip.

four Heat the oil for deep-frying in a deep-fryer or deep pan to 350°–375°F/180°–190°C, or until a cube of bread browns in 30 seconds. Pipe 5-inch/13-cm lengths about 3 inches/7.5 cm apart into the oil. Deep-fry for 2 minutes on each side, or until golden brown. Remove with a slotted spoon and drain on paper towels.

five Dust the churros with superfine sugar and cinnamon and serve.

recommended servings

Served either hot from the pan or cooled to room temperature, Churros go well with a cup of hot chocolate. They also make an elegant nibble with ordinary coffee or the Southwestern Coffee (see page 95).

These traditional, plain sweet fritters are served with their own flavored syrup in which they can be dunked or drenched. Maple syrup, corn syrup, or honey are good alternatives.

bunuelos with orange-cinnamon syrup

ingredients

1½ cups all-purpose flour, plus extra
  for dusting
1 tsp baking powder
¼ tsp salt
1 tbsp brown sugar
1 egg, beaten
2 tbsp butter, melted
about ½ cup evaporated milk
vegetable oil, for deep-frying

orange-cinnamon syrup
1½ cups water
grated rind of 1 small orange
4 tbsp freshly squeezed orange juice
½ cup brown sugar
1 tbsp honey
2 tsp ground cinnamon

one Sift the flour, baking powder, and salt together into a large bowl. Stir in the sugar. Beat in the egg and butter with enough evaporated milk to form a soft, smooth dough.

two Shape the dough into 8 balls. Cover and let rest for 30 minutes.

three Meanwhile, to make the syrup, place the water, orange rind and juice, sugar, honey, and cinnamon in a heavy-bottom pan over medium heat. Bring to a boil, stirring constantly, then reduce the heat and let simmer gently for 20 minutes, or until thickened.

four Flatten the dough balls to make cakes. Heat the oil for deep-frying in a deep-fryer or deep pan to 350–375°F/180–190°C, or until a cube of bread browns in 30 seconds. Deep-fry the bunuelos in batches for 4–5 minutes, turning once, or until golden brown and puffed. Remove with a slotted spoon and drain on paper towels. Serve with the syrup spooned over.

recommended servings
Serve these tempting fritters as a coffeetime sweet treat, or team with Southwestern Coffee (see page 95) for a late-night feast. They would also make a great dessert with scoops of good-quality vanilla ice cream.

prepare 20 minutes, plus 2½ hours' chilling
cook 10 minutes *serves* 4

When you want to chill out, literally, this ice-cold dessert will hit the spot. It couldn't be more elegant. To add a finishing touch, decorate with lime slices or twists or finely pared strips of rind.

guava, lime, and tequila sherbet

ingredients

scant 1 cup superfine sugar
scant 2 cups water
4 fresh ripe guavas or 8 canned
  guava halves

2 tbsp tequila
juice of ½ lime, or to taste
1 egg white

one Heat the sugar and water in a heavy-bottom pan over low heat until the sugar has dissolved. When the liquid turns clear, boil for 5 minutes, or until a thick syrup forms. Remove the pan from the heat and let cool.

two Cut the fresh guavas, if using, in half. Scoop out the flesh. Discard the seeds from the fresh or canned guava flesh. Transfer to a food processor or blender and process until smooth.

three Add the purée to the syrup with the tequila and lime juice to taste. Transfer the mixture to a freezerproof container and freeze for 1 hour, or until slushy.

four Remove from the freezer and process again until smooth. Return to the freezer and freeze until firm. Process again until smooth. With the motor still running, add the egg white through the feeder tube. Freeze until solid.

five Transfer the sherbet to the refrigerator 15 minutes before serving. Serve in scoops.

Note

Recipes using raw eggs should be avoided by infants, the elderly, pregnant women, convalescents, and anyone suffering from an illness.

recommended servings

A refreshing dessert to serve after some of the heavier-duty appetizers and main dishes, it goes well with other dishes, such as the Ceviche Salad (see page 11) or the Fish Fillets with Papaya Sauce (see page 37) for a light meal.

prepare 15–25 minutes, plus 15 minutes–2 hours'
processing or freezing
cook 10 minutes *serves* 4

Chocolate and chili are a classic southwestern combination with savory dishes, but can also be used together in sweet dishes. The chili just gives a warmth and richness to the chocolate.

chocolate chip and chili ice cream

ingredients

1 egg
1 egg yolk
generous ¼ cup superfine sugar
5½ oz/150 g semisweet chocolate,
  finely chopped
scant 2½ cups milk

1 dried red chili, such as ancho
1 vanilla bean
scant 2½ cups heavy cream
scant 1 cup semisweet, milk, or white
  chocolate chips

one Place the egg, egg yolk, and sugar in a heatproof bowl set over a pan of simmering water. Beat until light and fluffy.

two Place the chopped chocolate, milk, chili, and vanilla bean in a separate pan and heat gently until the chocolate has dissolved and the milk is almost boiling. Pour onto the egg mixture, discarding the chili and vanilla bean, and beat well. Let cool.

three Lightly whip the cream in a separate bowl. Fold into the cold mixture with the chocolate chips. Transfer to an ice cream machine and process for 15 minutes, or according to the manufacturer's instructions. Alternatively, transfer to a freezerproof container and freeze for 1 hour, or until partially frozen. Remove from the freezer, transfer to a bowl, and beat to break down the ice crystals. Freeze again for 30 minutes, then beat again. Freeze once more until firm.

four Transfer the ice cream to the refrigerator 15 minutes before serving. Serve in scoops.

Note

Recipes using raw eggs should be avoided by infants, the elderly, pregnant women, convalescents, and anyone suffering from an illness.

recommended servings

Reserve this rich dessert for serving after a middle-weight main course, such as the Tequila-Marinated Beef Steaks (see page 39), Chili-Shrimp Tacos (see page 41), or Chicken Fajitas (see page 43).

The name of these traditional Mexican cookies comes from the fact that they look like wedding bells, with their thick white coating of confectioners' sugar. The nuts can be chopped in a food processor.

mexican wedding cakes

ingredients

8 oz/225 g butter, softened

2 cups confectioners' sugar

1 tsp vanilla extract

1½ cups all-purpose flour, plus extra
  for dusting

½ tsp salt

⅞ cup pecan or walnut halves, toasted
  and finely chopped

one Cream the butter with half the sugar and vanilla extract in a large bowl. Sift the flour and salt together into the bowl and fold into the mixture. Stir in the nuts. Cover and let chill in the refrigerator for 1 hour, or until firm.

two Preheat the oven to 375°F/190°C. With floured hands, shape the dough into 1-inch/2.5-cm balls and place about 1½ inches/4 cm apart on 2 large baking sheets.

three Bake in the preheated oven for 10 minutes, or until set but not browned, rotating the baking sheets so that the cookies bake evenly. Let cool on the baking sheets for 2–3 minutes.

four Place the remaining sugar in a shallow dish. Roll the warm cookies in the sugar, then let cool on wire racks for 30 minutes. When cold, roll again in the sugar. Store in airtight containers.

recommended servings

These make a cheering sweet snack for midmorning or afternoon, are dainty enough to serve as part of a buffet-style meal and are also perfect after dinner with some Southwestern Coffee (see page 95).

Here we have a sweet alternative to the savory empanadas on page 21, this time with a creamy, fruity filling and a hint of crunchy nut. You could use apricots or mangoes in place of the peaches.

peach and pecan empanadas

ingredients

12 oz/350 g ready-made puff pastry, thawed if frozen

all-purpose flour, for dusting

3 fresh peaches

⅔ cup sour cream

4 tbsp brown sugar

4 tbsp pecan halves, toasted and finely chopped

beaten egg, to glaze

superfine sugar, for sprinkling

one Preheat the oven to 400°F/200°C. Roll out the pastry on a lightly floured counter. Using a 6-inch/15-cm saucer as a guide, cut out 8 circles.

two Place the peaches in a heatproof bowl and pour over enough boiling water to cover. Let stand for a few seconds, then drain and peel off the skins. Halve the peaches, remove the pits, and slice the flesh.

three Place a spoonful of sour cream on one half of each pastry circle and top with a few peach slices. Sprinkle over a little brown sugar and some nuts. Brush each edge with a little beaten egg, fold the pastry over the filling, and press the edges together to seal. Crimp the edges with a fork and prick the tops.

four Place on a baking sheet, brush with beaten egg, and sprinkle with superfine sugar. Bake in the preheated oven for 20 minutes, or until they turn golden brown.

recommended servings
These pastries are best served warm. Serve as a snack or a dessert after a southwestern main dish, such as Fish Fillets with Papaya Sauce (see page 37), to extend the fruity theme. Add some extra slices of fruit to decorate.

This is the drink that embodies the spirit of southwestern cooking—a fun-loving, sun baked lifestyle served up in a cocktail glass. Besides the classic concoction, there are fruit variations to be enjoyed.

margaritas

ingredients

classic margarita
crushed sea salt
1 lime wedge
handful of ice cubes, coarsely broken
3 tbsp tequila
3 tbsp freshly squeezed lime juice
1½ tbsp Cointreau
1 lime slice, to decorate

frozen mango margarita
superfine sugar
1 lime wedge
½ mango, peeled and chopped
3 tbsp tequila
3 tbsp freshly squeezed orange juice
1½ tbsp freshly squeezed lime juice
handful of crushed ice
1 orange slice, to decorate

CLASSIC MARGARITA

one To make the Classic Margarita, sprinkle a layer of salt onto a paper towel. Wipe the rim of a chilled cocktail or Margarita glass with the lime wedge, then invert onto the salt. Turn the glass upright, shaking off any excess salt.

two Place the broken ice cubes in a cocktail shaker, then add the tequila, lime juice, and Cointreau. Shake well, then strain into the prepared glass. Decorate with the lime slice and serve.

FROZEN MANGO MARGARITA

one To make the Frozen Mango Margarita, frost the rim of a large cocktail glass as in Step 1 of Classic Margarita but using sugar in place of the salt.

two Place the mango in a food processor or blender and process until smooth. Add the tequila, orange and lime juices, and crushed ice and blend until well combined but still slushy.

three Pour into the prepared glass, decorate with the orange slice, and serve.

recommended servings

Enjoy a Classic Margarita with Salsa (see pages 61–5), sour cream, and Guacamole (see page 59), and tortilla chips. Enjoy the Frozen Mango Margarita with warm sweet treats, such as bunuelos (see page 77).

Sultry sister to Tequila Sunrise, this is the ultimate cooler, fragrantly fruity yet with subtly discernible darker depths. And it looks every inch the part too.

tequila sunset

ingredients

1½ tbsp white rum
1½ tbsp tequila
⅓ cup freshly squeezed
  orange juice
1½ tbsp freshly squeezed lime juice

½ tall, straight-sided glass of
  crushed ice
1½ tbsp grenadine
pared spiral of lime rind, to decorate

one Place the white rum, tequila, orange and lime juices, and crushed ice in a cocktail shaker.

two Shake briefly, then pour the cocktail, with the ice, into the glass used to measure ice.

three Sprinkle the grenadine on top. Do not stir. Serve, decorated with a spiral of lime rind.

recommended servings

You can serve this drink with snacks such as Chicken and Corn Empanadas (see page 21) or Nachos (see page 23). It also goes well with main dishes such as Fish Fillets with Papaya Sauce (see page 37) or Tequila-Marinated Beef Steaks (see page 39).

This creamy yet tangy fruity cocktail is a real southwestern treat. Gold tequila is the standard drink matured in oak for a few years, during which time it mellows in flavor and turns golden in color.

acapulco

ingredients

1½ tbsp gold tequila
1½ tbsp dark rum
3 tbsp pineapple juice
1 tbsp freshly squeezed grapefruit juice

1½ tbsp coconut milk
½ Piña Colada glassful or tall, straight-sided glass of crushed ice
fresh pineapple wedges, to decorate

one Place the tequila, rum, pineapple and grapefruit juices, coconut milk, and crushed ice in a cocktail shaker.

two Shake well, then pour, with the ice, into the glass used to measure the ice.

three Spear the pineapple wedges onto a wooden toothpick and place across the top of the glass. Serve with straws.

recommended servings

A simple savory or sweet snack goes well with it, such as dried corn tortilla wedges (see Pork Tostadas, page 25) or tortilla chips with Pineapple and Mango Salsa (see page 65) and sour cream.

Perfect for a summer's day, the refreshingly fruity nature of Sangria belies its potency, so be careful not to overdo its consumption, although you can always reduce the alcohol content.

sangria

ingredients

1 bottle full-bodied red wine
3 tbsp Cointreau
3 tbsp brandy
juice of 1 orange and 1 lime
1 tbsp superfine sugar, or to taste
1 orange
1 lime
1 peach or red-skinned eating apple

to serve
1¼ cups club soda or lemonade
2 handfuls of ice cubes

one Pour the wine into a large pitcher or punch bowl. Add the Cointreau, brandy, and orange and lime juices, then stir in the sugar.

two Cover and let chill in the refrigerator for 2 hours.

three When ready to serve, cut the orange and lime into thin slices. Cut the peach in half, remove and discard the pit, and slice the flesh. Alternatively, cut the apple in half, remove and discard the core, and thinly slice. Remove the sangria from the refrigerator and stir in the sliced fruit.

four To serve, add the club soda and ice cubes, stir well, then pour or ladle into wine glasses.

recommended servings

This is perfect served at a stylish meal and makes a great accompaniment at an informal get-together with southwestern finger food, such as Chorizo and Cheese Quesadillas (see page 19) or Nachos (see page 23).

Kahlúa, Mexico's coffee-flavored liqueur, is teamed up with gold tequila in this luxurious afterdinner coffee. If you find the cream-floating finale too tricky, just whip the cream and spoon on top.

southwestern coffee

ingredients

1 tsp brown sugar, or to taste

2 tbsp Kahlúa or Tia Maria

1 tbsp gold tequila

⅔ cup hot black coffee

1–2 tbsp heavy cream

grated semisweet chocolate, to decorate

one Place the sugar, Kahlúa, and tequila in a warmed heatproof glass with a handle. Add the hot coffee and stir until the sugar has dissolved.

two Hold a teaspoon, back uppermost, just touching the surface of the coffee. Carefully pour the cream over the back of the spoon so that it floats on the surface.

three Sprinkle grated chocolate on top and serve at once.

recommended servings

Finish a southwestern feast with this sumptuous beverage. In a match made in heaven, both in looks and taste, serve with Mexican Wedding Cakes (see page 83) for a wicked treat any time of the day or night.

index